Omar BENCHAREF
Soulaimane KALOUN

HOW SMES CAN INNOVATE AND ACCELERATE GROWTH

Omar BENCHAREF
Soulaimane KALOUN

HOW SMES CAN INNOVATE AND ACCELERATE GROWTH

Generative AI and Machine Learning

ScienciaScripts

Cover image: www.ingimage.com

This book is a translation from the original published under ISBN 978-620-6-72841-2.

Publisher:
Sciencia Scripts
is a trademark of
Dodo Books Indian Ocean Ltd. and OmniScriptum S.R.L publishing group

120 High Road, East Finchley, London, N2 9ED, United Kingdom
Str. Armeneasca 28/1, office 1, Chisinau MD-2012, Republic of Moldova, Europe
Printed at: see last page
ISBN: 978-620-8-35350-6

ACKNOWLEDGEMENTS

We would like to express our deepest gratitude to all those who contributed, directly or indirectly, to the completion of this work.

First of all, our sincere thanks go to the Dean of the Marrakech Faculty of Science and Technology (FSTM), for his constant encouragement, support and invaluable advice throughout this project. His commitment and vision have been a source of inspiration for us.

We would also like to thank all our colleagues at UCAM for their collaboration, availability and constructive feedback, which greatly enriched this work. Their team spirit and support were essential at every stage.

Our thanks also go to the members of our small and large family, for their love, patience and unconditional support. You have been a driving force that has kept us determined and focused.

Finally, we would like to extend our warmest thanks to the Alidantec Inc. research centre for its invaluable support and resources, which played a decisive role in the success of this project. Your support enabled us to complete this work under the best possible conditions.

To all of you, we extend our deepest gratitude.

INTRODUCTION

AI AND SMES: A MARRIAGE OF REASON

Artificial intelligence (AI) has burst onto the business scene with unprecedented transformative potential. While large companies are investing massively in this technology to optimise their operations, cut costs and innovate on a massive scale, small and medium-sized enterprises (SMEs) can sometimes feel left behind. They face a number of challenges, including a lack of resources, qualified staff and sometimes even a clear strategic vision of how to integrate these innovations. Yet recent technological advances have made AI accessible, adaptable and financially viable, even for smaller organisations. That's where this book comes in.

This book sets out to demystify AI and show how it can be used pragmatically to meet the specific needs of SMEs. Far from requiring colossal investments or specialist teams, today's AI, and more specifically generative AI (GAI), is a versatile and intuitive tool. It can be implemented in almost every aspect of the business to optimise resources, improve productivity and drive innovation.

Why SMEs Can No Longer Ignore AI

SMEs play an essential role in the global economic fabric. They are a driving force behind job creation, local innovation and economic growth. However, they often have to compete with larger companies that have much greater financial, technical and human resources. This is where AI comes in as an equalising factor. By adopting AI, SMEs can automate repetitive tasks, analyse huge volumes of data in record time and make strategic decisions based on predictive analysis, without requiring an army of analysts or developers. The benefits don't stop there. Unlike other technologies that require a long time to learn and adapt, generative AI has become incredibly easy to use. Thanks to user-friendly interfaces, accessible online platforms and rapid integration with existing business tools, even less technical users can benefit. What's more, AI evolves with the business, learning from past interactions and adapting to future needs.

A Silent Revolution: How AI is Changing the Landscape of SMEs Beyond the efficiency gains, AI is redefining the very boundaries of what is possible for an SME. Today, a small service company can use AI to compete with giants by offering ultra-personalised customer experiences. A retailer can optimise its stocks and forecast sales with an accuracy that even

the big players sometimes struggle to achieve. A manufacturing company can automate its supply chain management and reduce production costs with just a few clicks.
Let's take the example of a human resources consultancy. Thanks to AI, it can analyse thousands of candidate profiles, suggest the best combinations of skills for a given team, and predict talent retention rates. What would have taken weeks of manual analysis can now be carried out in just a few minutes, with a precision and accuracy that are second to none.
greater objectivity. In this context, it is clear that AI is no longer just a competitive advantage, but a strategic necessity. SMEs that choose to ignore it risk quickly finding themselves outmatched, not only by their competitors, but also by the growing expectations of their customers and employees.

Generative AI: A Tool for Rapid Transformation

Among the various applications of AI, generative AI stands out for its ability to produce high-quality content from simple text instructions. It can create texts, images, videos and even product prototypes. This technology, which sometimes seems close to science fiction, is already a reality in many companies.

But what exactly is generative AI?

This is a branch of artificial intelligence that uses deep learning models to generate new content, based on existing models. For example, it can write articles, produce graphic designs, generate video scripts or create musical compositions. It's not just about creating: generative AI can also help formulate strategies, structure projects or even automate customer service.
The book itself benefited from the help of generative AI to structure its content, enrich its examples and refine its explanations. This process not only speeded up the writing process, but also ensured greater consistency and accuracy. AI has thus become a collaborator in its own right, a silent co-author who has helped to make this book a richer and more relevant guide.

The aims of this book This book is aimed at SME managers, entrepreneurs, operational managers and anyone who wants to understand how AI can be integrated into a business to optimise performance. Whether you are new to the subject or already familiar with the concepts of artificial intelligence, this book will provide you with :
• An overview of AI and generative AI technologies: understanding the fundamental concepts,

their concrete applications and the benefits they can bring to an SME.

- Practical examples: detailed case studies on the use of AI in various departments, including innovation, marketing, finance, and operations.
- An integration guide: how to assess your company's needs, select the right AI solutions and gradually integrate them into your day-to-day operations.
- An overview of future trends: What are the upcoming developments in the field of AI and how can SMEs prepare for them now?

Why This Book Is Different

Unlike other books that approach AI from a purely theoretical or technical point of view, this book has been designed with a pragmatic approach. Each concept is accompanied by concrete applications and solutions that can be adapted to the realities of SMEs. The emphasis is on action: at the end of each chapter, you will find clear recommendations and ready-to-implement strategies that you can adapt to your business.In short, this book is a comprehensive roadmap that will guide you step by step through the discovery and adoption of AI, to transform your SME into a more agile, innovative and successful business. Get ready to explore the fascinating world of AI and discover how it can revolutionise the way you work and run your business. Welcome to a new era where SMEs and AI become one to create a promising future together.

CHAPTER 1

UNDERSTANDING AI AND AI GENERATIVE

Artificial intelligence (AI) is a concept that can seem complex and intimidating to many people, particularly those from non-technology backgrounds. Yet it is increasingly present in our daily lives, often without us realising it. Whether it's through film recommendations on Netflix, shopping suggestions on Amazon or automatic replies in our emails, AI is making its way into our professional and personal lives [1].

But what does artificial intelligence really mean? And why is it so important for small and medium-sized enterprises (SMEs)? That's what we're going to find out in this chapter.

1.1 What is Artificial Intelligence?

AI refers to all the techniques that enable a machine to imitate certain human abilities, such as learning, reasoning, perception and even creativity [2]. Unlike traditional computer programmes that follow precise instructions, AI is designed to learn and adapt by analysing data.

In other words, AI is capable of :

- Analyse large amounts of data quickly.
- Learn from the data it processes.
- Make decisions based on what she has learned.

For example, AI can learn to identify trends in a company's sales or predict which products will be most in demand based on past data [3].

1.2 Why is AI important for SMEs?

AI is often associated with large technology companies, but it has many benefits for SMEs, including increasing productivity, improving decision-making and optimising operations [4]. Here are some reasons why SMEs should consider adopting AI:

1. Optimisation of resources: AI enables repetitive tasks to be automated, freeing up employees' time so that they can concentrate on higher value-added tasks.
2. Improved customer experience: Chatbots and virtual agents are able to answer frequently asked customer questions, handle complaints and offer round-the-clock support, even outside

normal working hours [5].
3. Cost reduction: Process automation reduces human error and operational costs, while increasing productivity.
4. Access to strategic information: by analysing data, AI can provide valuable insights into customer behaviour, market trends and product or service performance [6].

For example, a company specialising in e-commerce can use AI to personalise shopping recommendations to each customer based on their purchase history and preferences. This can lead to a significant increase in sales [7].

1.3 Generative AI: A New Dimension

Generative AI is a subset of artificial intelligence that focuses on creating original content. Unlike other types of AI that analyse data or make decisions based on existing models, generative AI can create new information, such as text, images or even videos, based on what it has learned.
How does it work? Generative AI uses deep learning algorithms, such as neural networks, to understand datasets and generate new output that is similar, but not identical, to the examples it has studied [8]. For example, a generative AI such as GPT-3 is capable of writing an entire article on a given topic by analysing millions of texts to extract structures and ideas [9].

1.4 APPLICATIONS OF GENERATIVE IA FOR SMES

Generative AI can be a major asset for SMEs, enabling them to produce quality content automatically and in record time. Here are a few concrete applications:

- Automated content writing: Whether writing blog posts, product descriptions or newsletters, generative AI can write content that reflects the company's style and tone [10].
- Creation of images or graphics: AI can generate bespoke visuals for marketing campaigns or publications on social networks.
- Product prototyping: Companies can use generative AI to design digital prototypes of new products before moving on to actual manufacturing [11].

These technologies, previously reserved for large companies, are now accessible thanks to the democratisation of AI solutions on the market. cloud and platforms such as OpenAI, Google Cloud AI and AWS Machine Learning [12]. This means that even SMEs with limited budgets can experiment and take advantage of AI to boost their growth.

CHAPTER 2

MASTERING PROMPT ENGINEERING WITH CHATGPT

Prompt Engineering is the art of formulating clear and effective instructions for interacting with an artificial intelligence model such as ChatGPT. This skill is crucial to getting the most out of generative AI. The more precise the wording of prompts, the more relevant and aligned the AI responses will be to your needs. This chapter explores how to design optimal prompts, create custom agents, and use ChatGPT to automate a variety of business tasks. We'll also look at concrete examples of use, best practice, and common mistakes to avoid for each application. By the end of this chapter, you'll be able to write effective prompts for different situations, automate report generation, analyse files, create tables, and even customise your own conversational agent.

2.1 INTRODUCTION TO PROMPT ENGINEERING

Prompt Engineering involves giving explicit instructions to an AI model to guide its responses. It's not just a matter of asking a question, but of guiding the AI with a clear context, specific constraints and a well-defined objective. For example:

- A bad prompt: Write an email for a client.
- A good prompt: Write a professional email to a dissatisfied customer about a late delivery, offering a discount on the next order.

The second prompt provides more context, enabling the AI to generate a more relevant response. Best practice: Be precise and clear. The more detailed your prompt, the better the response. Bad practice: Avoid vague or ambiguous instructions, as this can lead to irrelevant or imprecise answers.

2.2 EXAMPLES OF PROMPTS FOR CONCRETE USE CASES

2.2.1 Generate marketing content

Example 1: Writing a blog post on AI trends in 2024.

- Prompt: Write a 500-word article on trends in artificial intelligence in 2024. The article should include clear subheadings, recent statistics, and conclude with a perspective on the future

of AI.
• Expected result: The AI will write a structured article with relevant information and up-to-date data.
• What you shouldn't do: Write an article about AI. (Too general and the result risks being vague and uninformative).

Example 2: Writing a product description for an e-commerce site.
• Prompt: Write a detailed description of a new smartphone. Include technical specifications, user benefits and a short promotional sentence at the end.
• What not to do: Describe this phone. (Too vague and the result will probably be insufficient).

Best practice: Add constraints (text length, tone, type of information) to guide the AI.

2.2.2 File Analysis and Summarisation

AI can be used to analyse and summarise files such as financial reports, scientific articles or legal documents.

Example 1: Analysing a financial report.
• Prompt to use: Analyse this PDF file and summarise the company's three main financial strengths and three weaknesses. Also mentions the overall revenue trend compared with the previous year.
• What not to do: Summarise this document. (Not enough detail, the answer may lack depth).

Example 2: Creating tables from CSV data.
• Quick to use: Generates a summary table of monthly sales from this CSV file. Organises the columns by month and displays the totals for each product at the end of the table.
• What you shouldn't do: Create a table (no context, the table generated may not correspond to expectations).

Best practice: Indicate the desired output format (table, list, structured text) and the details you want to appear.

2.3 CREATE A AGENT CONVERSATIONAL AGENT WITH CHATGPT

A personalised conversational agent can help automate certain interactions with customers, employees or partners. To create a high-performance agent, it is essential to define its functions, response rules and tone.

Example of agent creation: Customer service for an online sales company.

1. Define the agent's role: You're a customer service agent for an online clothing shop. Your job is to answer questions about orders, provide information about returns and help customers track their parcels.
2. Establish common scenarios: What should I do if my parcel is late? How do I return a product? What are the delivery charges?
3. Create model responses: For each scenario, write model responses that the agent can adapt according to the context. Example:
    - If a customer asks how to track their parcel: "Hello, to track your order, please click on this link and enter your order number. If you have any further questions, I'm here to help!"
4. Define the agent's limits: You don't answer questions about the company's confidentiality policy. For these requests, transfer the conversation to a human.

What not to do: Do not specify the agent's limits, which may lead it to provide incorrect or inadequate information.

2.4 GOOD PRACTICE AND PITFALLS TO AVOID

1. Be specific in your instructions. Vague or poorly worded prompts can produce irrelevant responses.

- What to do: Explain precisely what you expect, providing the necessary context.
- What not to do: Ask for answers without specifying the desired length, tone or format.

2. Use concrete examples. Showing the AI what you expect can greatly improve the quality of responses.

- What to do: Present a model or example to guide the AI (for example, provide a sample paragraph if you want a response in the same style).
- What not to do: Let the AI guess the style or format.

3. Break complex tasks down into simpler steps. If your task is complex, break it down into several simpler prompts.

- What to do: First, ask for a data analysis, then ask for a summary of this analysis.
- What not to do: Try to get everything in a single request.

2.5 GENERATE DES TABLES AND VISUALIZATIONS WITH CHATGPT

AI can also generate tables and basic visualisations from structured data.

Example: Generate a sales table.

- Prompt to use: Creates a summary table of monthly sales for products A, B and C. The columns should include the month, product, unit sales and total revenue. At the end, add a total line for each product.

Expected result:

Month	Product	Sales (Units)	Total income
January	A	100	2000 €
January	B	50	1250 €
February	A	80	1600 €
February	C	40	800 €
Total		270	5650 €

What not to do: Ask for a table without specifying the columns, which could lead to a disorganised result.

2.6 ANALYSE FILES AND GENERATE REPORTS

ChatGPT can also analyse files, whether CSV, PDF or simple text documents, to generate reports and summaries.

Example: Summarising a PDF report on quarterly performance.

- Prompt: Read this PDF file and write a one-page summary of the company's quarterly performance. Focus on the key figures (growth, profit, etc.) and mention the challenges encountered.

What not to do: Read this file and tell me what you think. (Too general and the answer may not cover the important points).

Best practice: Specify the specific sections or information you want to see in the summary.

2.7 CONCLUSION : OPERATE THE FULL POTENTIAL OF PROMPT ENGINEERING

Prompt Engineering is an essential skill for interacting effectively with AI. By mastering this art, you'll be able to optimise your interactions with models like ChatGPT, automate content creation, generate reports and create high-performance conversational agents. Remember that clarity, precision and experimentation are the keys to designing successful prompts. By applying good practice and avoiding common mistakes, you'll be able to harness the full potential of generative AI to meet your business needs.

CHAPTER 3

TRANSFORMING MARKETING WITH AI

Artificial intelligence is revolutionising marketing, opening up new possibilities for companies to analyse data, personalise customer experiences and improve their campaigns. This chapter will guide you step-by-step through how to use AI in your marketing, with concrete examples and case studies based on data files you can manipulate directly. We will cover practical usage scenarios, such as analysing customer segmentation, personalising marketing campaigns, automatically generating reports and dashboards, and evaluating campaign performance.

3.1 AI for marketing: a radical transformation

AI is increasingly being used to transform marketing processes, mainly thanks to its ability to:

- Rapidly analyse massive volumes of data.
- Automate repetitive tasks such as generating content, analysing customer behaviour or creating reports.
- Predict trends and tailor recommendations to each customer's needs and preferences.

SMEs, which do not always have dedicated in-house marketing resources, can benefit from these technologies to compete with large companies. AI enables small organisations to take advantage of advanced analyses and optimise their marketing strategy without a huge investment in staff or technology.

3.2 Using AI for customer segmentation

Aim: Understand how to use AI to segment customers according to their buying behaviour, demographics and preferences, based on real data.

CASE STUDY: SEGMENTING CUSTOMERS BY INCOME AND EXPENDITURE SCORE

1. Download the file: customers_data.csv.
2. File description :

o Customer_ID: Unique customer identifier.

o Age: Customer's age.

o Gender: Customer's gender.

o Annual_Income: Customer's annual income in euros.

o Spending_Score: Customer spending score (subjective evaluation from 1 to 100 based on purchasing habits).

3. Objective: Segment customers into three groups:

o Low income: Less than €40,000.

o Average income : Between €40,000 and €60,000.

o High income: More than €60,000.

Prompt analysis :

arduino Copy code

Read the 'customers_data.csv' file and divide the customers into three segments based on annual income: 'Low Income', 'Middle Income' and 'High Income'. Calculate the average spend score for each segment and generate a summary table showing the number of customers per segment, the average annual income, and the average spend score.

Expected result:

Segment	Number of Customers	Annual Income Medium	Spend Score Medium
Low income	3	36 000 €	65
Income medium	4	50 000 €	72
High income	3	67 000 €	80

4. Interpreting the results: Identify which segment has the highest spend score. You can direct your marketing efforts towards this group or identify strategies to increase the spend score of segments with a lower score.

What you need to do: Specify the type of segmentation and the indicators to be used (in this case, income and expenditure score).

What not to do: Ask for a simple segmentation without providing specific criteria, which could lead to inconsistent results.

3.3 Automated personalisation of marketing campaigns

Aim: To create personalised marketing campaigns based o n previously identified customer segments.

CASE PRACTICE: CUSTOMISATION OF MARKETING OFFERS FOR EACH SEGMENT

1. Objective: Generate specific marketing offers for each customer segment.
2. Example of Prompt :

Create three personalised promotional emails for each customer segment identified above ("Low income", "Middle income", "High income"). Each email must include a specific offer corresponding to the segment's budget and spending habits, and must contain an invitation to take advantage of a time-limited promotion.

Expected result:

• Email for the "Low Income" segment: Special offer on affordable products with a 10% discount coupon on future orders.

• Email for the "Middle Income" segment: Promotion on popular products with free delivery on the next order.

• Email for the "High Income" segment: Exclusive access to new products with a 15% discount for purchases over €500.

3. Interpretation: Use these emails to launch automated marketing campaigns on platforms such as MailChimp or HubSpot, while measuring the response of each segment to refine future campaigns.

What you need to do: Tailor the tone and content of each email to the target segment to maximise engagement.

What not to do: Send the same content to all segments, which will reduce the effectiveness of the campaign.

3.4 Marketing Performance Analysis with AI

AI can be used to generate analytical dashboards and monitor campaign performance in real time.

CASE PRACTICAL : GENERATE A TABLE OF DASHBOARD OF CAMPAIGN PERFORMANCE

1. Download the file: campaign_data.csv.

2. File description :

o Campaign_ID: Unique identifier for the campaign.

o Campaign_Name: Name of the campaign.

o Start_Date: Campaign start date.

o End_Date: End date of the campaign.

o Total_Sales: Total sales generated by the campaign.

o ROI (%): Return on investment as a percentage.

3. Objective: Create a summary table of campaign performance, calculating the total sales generated by all campaigns, the average ROI and the best-performing campaign.

Prompt analysis :
Analyses the 'campaign_data.csv' file and creates a summary table showing the total sales of all campaigns, the average ROI and identifies which campaign achieved the best return on investment. It also provides suggestions for improving the performance of future campaigns.

Expected result:
- Total sales: €109,000

- Average ROI: 158

- Best-performing campaign : Year-End Clearance with a ROI of 210%.

4. AI suggestions: Launch campaigns similar to "Year-End Clearance" with a more attractive offer for highly committed customers.

What you need to do: Specify the key performance indicators (sales, ROI) you want to analyse.

What not to do: Ask for a simple analysis without indicating the KPIs, which could give an incomplete view of performance.

3.5 Automated Generation of Marketing Reports

AI can automatically generate marketing reports to present the results of campaigns and initiatives.

CASE PRACTICALN: CREATION OF A REPORT QUARTERLY REPORT

1. Objective: To generate a quarterly report summarising the performance of marketing campaigns.
2. Example of Prompt :

Produce a quarterly report based on the data in the 'campaign_data.csv' file. The report should include an introduction, a section on campaign performance with trend graphs, and a conclusion with recommendations for the next quarter. Expected result: A clearly structured report, including key information on campaign performance and suggestions for future strategies. What you need to do: Provide clear instructions on the structure and content of the report. What not to do: Request a report without specifying the information to be included, which may result in an incomplete document.

3.6 Conclusion: AI, an Indispensable Asset for SME Marketing

AI is much more than just a tool for large companies. By learning how to use it, even SMEs can transform their marketing strategies, segment their customer base more finely, personalise their campaigns and analyse performance with unrivalled accuracy. By combining automation and advanced analytics, AI enables SMEs to make informed decisions, better target their customers and optimise their resources to achieve maximum results with minimum effort. These case studies show that AI is accessible to businesses of all sizes and can be implemented without the need for advanced technical skills. Using the data files and prompts provided, you can experiment directly with AI and discover for yourself how it can transform your marketing operations.Feel free to explore further by adjusting the prompts to your specific needs and integrating your own data to get the most out of AI in your business.

CHAPTER 4

REVOLUTIONISING CORPORATE FINANCE WITH AI

Chapter objective: This chapter focuses on the use of artificial intelligence to automate, analyse and optimise financial processes in SMEs. We will discuss practical applications such as financial prediction, performance analysis, automation of accounting tasks, and cash flow management. The chapter will conclude with practical case studies with downloadable example files for practice.

4.1 Why is AI Crucial for SME Finance?

Financial management is an area where every detail counts. Human errors can lead to considerable financial losses, and optimising resources is crucial to the survival and growth of SMEs. AI offers innovative solutions to overcome these challenges by enabling:

- Predictive analysis: predict cash flow, sales and cost trends with a high degree of accuracy.
- Task automation: Reduce errors by automating accounting tasks such as invoicing, bank reconciliation and financial reporting.
- Data-driven decision-making: Helping executives make informed decisions by providing comprehensive, real-time analysis.

4.2 AI applications in Finance

AI can be applied to several aspects of corporate finance:

1. Cash Flow Prediction

- o Use predictive models to anticipate cash flow fluctuations.
- o Anticipate periods of tight cash flow and propose mitigation strategies.

2. Cost optimisation

- o Analyse company expenditure to identify areas where costs can be reduced.
- o Detect inefficiencies in internal processes.

3. Automation of accounting tasks

- o Automate invoice entry, account reconciliation and report generation.
- o Reduce the time needed for repetitive administrative tasks.

4. Financial Performance Evaluation

- Create dynamic dashboards to assess the performance of different departments.
- Monitor key performance indicators (KPIs) in real time.

4.3 Financial prediction with AI

CASE STUDY: PREDICTING CASH FLOWS

1. Download the file: sales_data.csv.
2. File description :

- Month: Month of the year.
- Product_A_Sales, Product_B_Sales, Product_C_Sales: Monthly sales of each product.
- Revenue: Total sales per month.

3. Objective: Use this file to predict revenues for the next three months.

Prompt analysis :

Read the 'sales_data.csv' file and predict the next three months' revenues for the company. Use past monthly trends to estimate revenue growth or decline. Also provides an estimate of total revenue per month for each product.

Expected result: A predictive revenue table with estimates for each product:

Month	Product_A_Sales	Product_B_Sales	Product_C_Sales	Total income
January	210	180	160	5500 €
February	215	185	165	5650 €
March	220	190	170	5800 €

4. Interpreting the results: Use these forecasts to adjust your budgets and plan future expenditure.

What needs to be done: Provide information on historical trends to help AI build an accurate predictive model. Don'ts: Failure to include sufficient context or history can limit the accuracy of predictions.

4.4 Automation of accounting tasks

CASE STUDY: AUTOMATING INVOICE GENERATION

1. Objective: Automatically generate invoices based on monthly sales data.
2. Example of Prompt :

From the 'sales_data.csv' file, generate monthly invoices for products A, B and C. Each invoice must include the month, the product, the quantity sold, the unit price and the total amount.

Expected result: Detailed invoices for each product, with the following information:

Invoice ID	Month	Product	Quantity Sold	Prices Unitary	Amount Total
F001	January	A	100	20 €	2000 €
F002	January	B	90	15 €	1350 €
F003	February	A	120	20 €	2400 €
F004	February	B	95	15 €	1425 €

3. Interpretation: Use these invoices to automate accounts receivable management and payments.

What you need to do: Specify the invoice format and the information to be included.

What not to do: Failure to define the format could result in incomplete or incorrect invoices.

4.5 Evaluating Financial Performance with Dynamic Dashboards

CASE PRACTICE : GENERATE A TABLE OF PERFORMANCE PERFORMANCE SCORECARD

1. Download the file: campaign_data.csv.
2. File description :

o Campaign_ID: Campaign identifier.

o Total_Sales: Sales generated by the campaign.

o ROI (%): Return on investment for the campaign.

3. Objective: Create a dashboard to monitor the financial performance of each campaign.

Example of Prompt :

Read the 'campaign_data.csv' file and generate a dashboard showing total sales per campaign, average ROI, and a comparison of campaign performance. Displays everything in table form with coloured indicators (green for campaigns with an ROI of over 150% and red for those below 100%).

Expected result:

Campaign_ID	Campaign	Total Sales	KING (%)	Indicator of Performance
101	Spring Sale	15 000 €	120%	
102	Summer Promotion	22 000 €	150%	
103	Back to School	18 000 €	130%	
104	Holiday Deals	24 000 €	180%	
105	Year-End Clearance	30 000 €	210%	

4. Interpretation: Identify the best-performing campaigns and allocate more budget to future similar campaigns.

What you need to do: Use visual indicators to help you assess performance. What not to do: Create a table without visual indicators, which would make reading and analysis more complex.

4.6 Sales Forecast Automation

Automating sales forecasts is essential for SMEs that want to manage their stocks, plan production and align their revenue targets.

CASE STUDY: AUTOMATING SALES FORECASTS

1. Objective: Automate sales forecasting for products A, B and C.

2. Example of Prompt :

Uses data from the 'sales_data.csv' file to create a predictive model that estimates sales of products A, B and C for the next quarter. Also provides a graph showing sales trends over the last six months and forecasts.

Expected result: A graph showing sales trends, with forecasts for the coming months.MWhat you need to do: Include a sales history to build a solid forecasting model. Don'ts: Failure to provide sufficient historical data limits the accuracy of forecasts.

4.7 Conclusion: Leveraging AI for Optimal Financial Management

AI is a powerful tool for improving financial management in SMEs. By automating repetitive tasks, accurately analysing performance and predicting cash flows, AI enables finance managers to make strategic decisions and focus on higher value-added activities. By applying the case studies in this chapter, you will be able to revolutionise your financial operations and maximise your company's profitability.

CHAPTER 5

AUTOMATING BUSINESS TASKS WITH AI

Chapter objective: This chapter explores how SMEs can leverage artificial intelligence to automate their administrative, management, and day-to-day operational tasks. We will discuss practical scenarios for using automation, including email management, automated reporting, customer request processing, and robotic process automation (RPA). At the end of the chapter, you will find example files and prompts that you can use to test the automation of certain tasks yourself.

5.1 Why automate business tasks?

Automation enables companies to reduce human error, speed up repetitive processes and free up employees' time to focus on more strategic activities. For SMEs, automation is a major asset, saving time and resources while improving the quality and consistency of results.

Benefits of automation :

- Reduced errors: Fewer human errors thanks to the automation of repetitive tasks.
- Time savings: Automating tasks generally takes much less time than carrying them out manually.
- Increased productivity: Employees can concentrate on higher value-added tasks.
- Improved quality: Automated processes are uniform, guaranteeing consistency.

5.2 Email and Communication Automation

CASE PRACTICAL : ANSWER AUTOMATIC TO EMAILS

1. Objective: Automate responses to routine emails (requests for quotes, order tracking, etc.).
2. Download the example file: email_templates.csv (File containing email response templates for different scenarios).
3. File description :

   - Scenario: Type of request received by email (e.g. Quote request, Order tracking, Question about a product).
   - Template_Response: Standard response to be sent.

Example of Prompt :

Uses the 'email_templates.csv' file and automatically generates responses for each type of request listed. Sends a response according to the corresponding scenario, e.g. for a request for a quote, uses the appropriate response template.

Expected result: A set of automatically generated emails for each type of request, ready to be sent, for example :

- Quote request: Hello, thank you for your interest. Please find attached our personalised quotation. Please do not hesitate to contact us if you have any further questions.
- Order tracking: Hello, your order has been dispatched and is on its way. You can track your parcel by clicking on this link: [tracking link]. Thank you for your confidence.

What you need to do: Prepare response models for common scenarios to ensure rapid and consistent responses. What you shouldn't do: Reply manually to each email when a template can be used to automate replies.

5.3 Automated Report Creation

CASE STUDY: AUTOMATED GENERATION OF WEEKLY REPORTS

1. Objective: To generate weekly reports on the company's performance.
2. Download the file: weekly_performance.csv.
3. File description :

  - Week: Week of the year.
  - Total_Sales: Total sales achieved during the week.
  - New_Customers: Number of new customers.
  - Customer_Complaints : Number of customer complaints.

Example of Prompt :

Read the 'weekly_performance.csv' file and generate a weekly report showing total sales, number of new customers, and customer complaints. Use this information to create a summary with graphs and trend analysis for the last four weeks.

Expected result: An automated report containing the following information:

- Weekly performance table.
- Graphs showing changes in sales, new customers and complaints.
- Trend analysis: Comparison of weekly performance with the previous four weeks.

What you need to do: Specify the indicators to be analysed (sales, customer complaints) and the type of display required (graph, table).

What not to do: Failure to specify key indicators could result in an incomplete or unhelpful report.

5.4 Automated processing of customer requests

CASE STUDY: MANAGING PRODUCT RETURN REQUESTS

1. Objective: Automate the process of handling return requests.
2. Download the example file: returns_requests.csv.
3. File description :

○ Request_ID: Unique identifier for the return request.

○ Customer_ID: Identifier of the customer who made the request.

○ Product_Name: Name of the product to be returned.

○ Return_Reason: Reason for return (e.g. Defective product, Wrong size, Does not match description).

Example of Prompt :

Read the 'returns_requests.csv' file and automate the processing of each returns request. For each request, generate a response indicating the returns procedure according to the reason for the return. If the product is faulty, include an offer of a free replacement.

Expected result: A set of automatically generated responses for each return request, for example :

- Defective product: Hello, we're sorry for the inconvenience. Please return the faulty product to us using the enclosed returns label. We will send you a replacement product as soon as we receive it.

• Wrong size: Hello, we accept your return. You are welcome to
choose a new size using our online returns form. Please return the actual product with the attached label. What needs to be done: Define processing rules according to the reasons for return.

What not to do: Apply the same generic response to all requests, which could damage the customer experience.

5.5 Robotic Process Automation (RPA) for SMEs

Robotic Process Automation (RPA) is software that automates repetitive tasks in business processes, such as data extraction, automatic data entry or report generation.

CASE STUDY: AUTOMATING DATA ENTRY

1. Objective: Automate customer order entry in an ERP system.
2. Download the file: customer_orders.csv.
3. File description :

- o Order_ID: Unique identifier for the order.
- o Customer_Name: Customer name.
- o Product_Name: Name of the product ordered.
- o Quantity: Quantity ordered.
- o Order_Date: Order date.

Example of Prompt :
Read the 'customer_orders.csv' file and automate the entry of each order in the company's ERP system. Each order must be recorded with the customer ID, product name, quantity and order date. Expected result: An automated process that registers each order in the ERP system in a matter of seconds.What you need to do: Ensure that the file format corresponds to the input requirements of the ERP system. What not to do: Don't check the data format, which could lead to integration errors in the ERP system.

5.6 Conclusion: Automation, an essential ally for SMEs

Automating tasks is an opportunity for SMEs to optimise their processes, reduce human error and free up employee time. By applying the case studies in this chapter, you will be able to simplify your operations and increase your company's overall efficiency. These examples show you how to use AI and RPA to transform manual tasks into automated processes, ensuring greater productivity. Feel free to experiment with your own data and adapt the prompts to meet the specific needs of your business.

CHAPTER 6

INTELLIGENT AGENTS AND VIRTUAL TEAM MANAGEMENT

Chapter objective: This chapter focuses on the use of intelligent agents to automate the management of virtual teams and improve the operational efficiency of SMEs. We'll explore how to create, customize, and deploy intelligent agents in different contexts: customer service, project management, and team collaboration. Each section includes detailed instructions and Python code that readers can follow to simulate and test the functionality of intelligent agents themselves.

6.1 What is an Intelligent Agent?

An intelligent agent is an AI program designed to perform specific tasks autonomously or semi-autonomously. Unlike traditional chatbots, intelligent agents can learn from their interactions, adapt to user needs and integrate with various systems to perform more complex tasks.

EXAMPLES OF INTELLIGENT AGENTS :

- Customer service agent: Answers customers' questions, resolves simple problems and escalates more complex requests.
- Project management agent: tracks the progress of tasks, sends automatic reminders and updates project status.
- Team coordinator: Facilitates communication between team members, plans meetings and generates reports automatically.

6.2 Create a Customer Service Agent

PRACTICAL EXAMPLE 1: CREATING A CUSTOMER SERVICE AGENT

Aim: To set up an agent capable of answering customers' routine questions about products, orders and returns.

Step 1: Prepare the data file

- Download the FAQ_client.csv file.

• The file contains two columns:

o Question: Questions frequently asked by customers (e.g. "What is the delivery time?").

o Response: Corresponding answer to each question.

Step 2: Configure the Python script for the agent Create a Python script with the following code to read the file and configure the customer service agent.

```
import pandas as pd

# Upload the CSV file containing the questions and answers
faq_file = 'FAQ_client.csv' # Replace with the path to your CSV file
faq_df = pd.read_csv(faq_file)

# Function for obtaining the answer based on the question asked
def get_response(question):
    # Search for the corresponding response in the CSV file for
    index, row in faq_df.iterrows():
        if row['Question'].lower() in question.lower():
            return row['Response']
    # If the question is not found, return a generic "I'm not sure I can
    answer this question, I'll just
forward your request to a human agent."

# Test the agent with a question
question_test = "What is the delivery time?"
print(f "Question : {question_test}") print(f
"Answer : {get_answer(question_test)}")
```

Step 3: Testing the agent

• Run the script and ask the various questions contained in the FAQ_client.csv file.

• Modify the questions to test the agent's answers.

Step 4: Add personalised responses

• Edit the FAQ_client.csv file to add new questions and answers.

• Re-test the agent with the new information.

Expected result: The agent must automatically answer common questions using the information provided in the CSV file. If the question is not in the file, it must escalate the request to a human operator.Tip: Experiment by asking questions that are not in the file to check the agent's ability to escalate requests.

6.3 Create a Project Management Agent

PRACTICAL EXAMPLE 2: AUTOMATING TEAM COORDINATION

Aim: To create a project management agent capable of tracking the progress of tasks, sending reminders and generating progress reports.

Step 1: Prepare project information

• Create an Excel file named project_tasks.csv with the following columns:

o Task_ID: Unique identifier for the task.

o Task_Description: Description of the task.

o Assigned_To: Name of the employee assigned to the task.

o Due_Date: Due date.

o Status: Current status of the task (In progress, Completed, Late).

Step 2: Configure the Python script for the agent Create a Python script with the following code to read the file, send reminders by email and generate a report.

```
import pandas as pd import smtplib
from email.mime.text import MIMEText
from email.mime.multipart import MIMEMultipart from datetime import datetime
# Configure email sending
EMAIL_USER = "votre_email@gmail.com" # Replace with your email
EMAIL_PASSWORD = "your_password" # Replace with your password
# Load the CSV file containing the tasks
tasks_file = 'project_tasks.csv' # Replace with the path to your CSV file tasks_df =
pd.read_csv(tasks_file)
# Filter late tasks today = datetime.now().date()
tasks_df['Due_Date'] = pd.to_datetime(tasks_df['Due_Date']).dt.date late_tasks =
tasks_df[(tasks_df['Due_Date'] < today) & (tasks_df['Status'] != 'Completed')]
# Prepare and send emails to those responsible for overdue tasks def send_email(to_email,
subject, body):
msg = MIMEMultipart() msg['From'] = EMAIL_USER msg['To'] = to_email msg['Subject'] =
subject
```

msg.attach(MIMEText(body, 'plain'))

try:

with smtplib.SMTP('smtp.gmail.com', 587) as server: server.starttls() server.login(EMAIL_USER,EMAIL_PASSWORD)server.sendmail(EMAIL_USER, to_email, msg.as_string()) print(f "Email sent to {to_email}")

```
    except Exception as e:
        print(f "Error sending email: {e}")

# Send reminders for each late task for index,
row in late_tasks.iterrows():
    recipient_email = f"{row['Assigned_To']}@exemple.com" # Make sure that
the email address matches the user
    task_description = row['Task_Description']
    due_date =
    row['Due_Date'].strftime('%d/%m/%Y')

    email_subject = "Late Task Reminder
    email_body = f "Hello, the task '{task_description}' was due on
{due_date} and has not yet been completed. Please complete it as soon as
possible."
```

Step 3: Automate daily execution

• Configure a cron job (under Unix) or a cloud service (AWS Lambda, Google Cloud) to run the script every day at 9.00am.

• Use the following code to schedule daily execution:

```
# Open the crontab with the following command in the terminal
crontab -e

# Add this line to run the script every day at 9.00 a.m.
0 9 * * * /usr/bin/python3 /path/to/your_script.py
```

Step 4: Test the script

• Modify the task dates in project_tasks.csv to simulate delays.

• Run the script and check that the emails are sent correctly.

Expected result: The agent automatically sends reminders for each overdue task.

Tip: Add a feature that generates a weekly report from this script to monitor overall progress.

6.4 Automate Meeting Management

PRACTICAL EXAMPLE 3: AUTOMATING MEETINGS

Goal: Set up an agent capable of scheduling meetings, sending invitations and generating minutes.Step 1: Prepare the meetings file

- Download the meeting_schedule.csv file or create a file with the following columns:
  - Meeting_ID: Meeting identifier.
  - Date: Date of the meeting.
  - Time: Time of the meeting.
  - Participants : List of participants.
  - Agenda : Points to be discussed during the meeting.

Step 2: Configure the Python script for the agent Create a Python script with the following code to read the file, send invitations and generate reports.

```
# Script similar to the previous example but adapted to manage meetings
# Use a similar format to plan meetings and send minutes.
```

Step 3: Automate execution

- Use a cron job or a cloud automation service to run the script before each meeting.

Conclusion: Practice makes perfect

By following these practical examples, you will be able to create, customise and test intelligent agents to automate various processes within your SME. Feel free to experiment with these scripts and adapt them to your needs to maximise the effectiveness of your intelligent agents.

CHAPTER 7

UNLEASHING THE POTENTIAL OF GENERATIVE AI FOR INNOVATION AND BRAINSTORMING

Chapter objective: This chapter explores how generative AI (GAI) can be used to stimulate innovation and enrich brainstorming sessions within SMEs. We will demonstrate how ChatGPT can act as a creative catalyst, play a variety of roles in simulated discussions and deliver balanced ideas by simulating complex scenarios. Practical examples and prompt engineering techniques will enable you to set up virtual brainstorming sessions and integrate generative AI into your innovation processes.

7.1 Why use Generative AI in Innovation Sessions?

Innovation is the engine of growth for businesses of all sizes. However, it can be difficult to think outside the box and generate truly new ideas. That's where generative AI comes in. Capable of processing complex information and producing original content, it can explore new concepts, simulate creative scenarios and offer fresh perspectives.

Benefits ofusing Generative AI forinnovation :

- Divergent thinking: AI generates a variety of ideas that go beyond human cognitive biases.
- Continuous brainstorming: It can operate in brainstorming mode 24 hours a day, without fatigue or creative blockages.
- Staging discussions: The AI can play different roles during simulated discussions to offer a variety of viewpoints.
- Scenario simulation: It can simulate business scenarios, discussions between departments and role-playing games.

7.2 Prompt Engineering techniques for Brainstorming with ChatGPT

To get the most out of generative AI in brainstorming, it's essential to master Prompt Engineering. Here are a few techniques and examples for configuring ChatGPT effectively during your innovation sessions.

PRACTICAL EXAMPLE 1: CREATING ROLE-PLAYING GAMES TO SIMULATE INNOVATION SCENARIOS

Aim: To set up a simulated discussion between several agents (e.g. financial agent, HR agent, innovation agent) to evaluate a project idea from different angles.

Step 1: Configure the basic prompt Create a prompt that defines the context and roles of each agent.

```
**Prob:**
You're ChatGPT and you'll be playing the role of several agents within
the company. Here are the roles you'll play:

1. **Financial Officer**: Focuses on the profitability and financial
viability of projects.
2. **HR Officer**: Defends the impact of projects on employees and their
well-being.
3. **Innovation Officer**: Proposes new ideas and identifies growth
opportunities.

The context: The company wants to launch a new product. Each of you must
evaluate this proposal from your own point of view and take part in a
discussion to reach a balanced decision.

Start the discussion!
```

Step 2: Leading the virtual brainstorming session

• Run the prompt and let the AI generate a simulated discussion between the agents.

• In each round, the agents have to defend their point of view and put forward specific arguments.

Example of Result :

Financial Officer: "This new product is interesting, but its development cost is high. We should consider reducing the functionality or increasing the selling price to ensure a rapid return on investment."HR Officer: "Reducing functionality could lead to an overload of work for the development team and reduce their motivation. It's important to consider the impact on human resources."Innovation Officer: "We could envisage a phased launch, starting with a minimum viable product. This would allow us to test the market while minimising initial costs."

Stage 3: Concluding the discussion

• Ask ChatGPT to summarise the discussion and propose a balanced solution that takes account of each agent's point of view.

Example of Prompt :

```
Summary of the discussion: Propose a solution that takes into account
financial viability, employee well-being and innovation. Propose an action
plan.
```

Expected result: A solution that balances the priorities of the various agents, ready to be discussed in greater detail at a meeting.

What needs to be done: Define clear roles and provide a clear context for discussion.

What not to do: Allow the discussion to proceed without structure or direction, which can lead to confusion of roles and a loss of coherence.

7.3 Using Generative AI to Generate Product and Service Ideas

Generative AI can be used to generate ideas for products and services based on market trends and consumer preferences.

PRACTICAL EXAMPLE 2: GENERATING PRODUCT IDEAS BASED ON TRENDS

Aim: To use AI to generate product ideas based on current trends.

Step 1: Prepare the basic prompt Create a prompt that defines the context and criteria for generating ideas.

```
**Prob:**
ChatGPT, I want to launch a new product in the consumer technology sector.
Here are the criteria to consider:

1. The product must be based on current technological trends (e.g. IoT,
artificial intelligence, mobility).
2. It must respond to growing consumer needs (e.g. reduced energy
consumption, connectivity, health).
3. Come up with five product ideas based on these criteria, with a brief
description of each product.

Get the ideas rolling!
```

Example of Result :

1. AI Sensor for Home Energy Savings: An intelligent sensor that integrates with heating and air conditioning systems to optimise energy consumption according to occupant habits.
2. Connected Health Tracking Watch: A connected watch that analyses stress levels and suggests relaxation exercises in real time.
3. Mobile Personal Assistant for Cars: An AI-based personal assistant for cars that predicts routes, identifies the nearest service stations and offers maintenance suggestions.
4. Office Wellness Application: An application that monitors posture and productivity at work, and suggests active breaks to avoid a sedentary lifestyle.
5. AI Coaching Platform for Personal Development: An AI platform that offers personalised skills development and coaching programmes.

Step 2: Evaluate the ideas generated

- Ask the AI to evaluate each idea according to different criteria (e.g. development cost, market potential, technical feasibility).

Prompt for assessment :

```
Evaluate each idea according to the following criteria:
1. Development cost (Low, Medium, High).
2. Market potential (Low, Medium, High).
3. Technical feasibility (Low, Medium, High).

Rank ideas according to their overall potential.
```

Expected result: A detailed assessment of each product idea, with a recommendation of the one with the greatest potential. What you need to do: Include clear evaluation criteria to help the AI sort through the ideas. What not to do: Generate ideas without specifying success criteria, which could produce unrealistic results.

7.4 Create Hypothetical Scenarios to Simulate the Impact of Innovations

Hypothetical scenarios are used to test the potential impact of new ideas or innovations before they are implemented.

EXAMPLE PRACTICE 3 : SIMULATION OF SCENARIOS FOR PRODUCT LAUNCHES

Aim: To use AI to simulate the impact of a new product on the market.

Step 1: Configure the prompt

- Define the basic assumptions (e.g. product, price, target market).

```
**Prob:**
Simulate the impact of the launch of a new product (Mobile Personal
Assistant for Cars) on the European market. Take into account the following
elements:

1. Price: €150.
2. Target market: Drivers aged between 25 and 45 who use connected
technologies.
3. Competitors : GPS devices and navigation applications.
```

Example of Result :

- Estimated monthly sales: 10,000 units in the first month, growing by 5% a month.
- Potential challenges: Competition from free applications, need to educate the market about how to use the product.

Step 2: Analysing the results

- Adjust assumptions to test different scenarios (e.g. higher price, new target market).

What you need to do: Clearly define the assumptions and scenarios to be simulated.

What not to do: Leave the scenario without clear assumptions, which could lead to irrelevant results.

7.5 Conclusion: Generative AI, a Pillar of Innovation

Generative AI offers immense potential for stimulating innovation and generating new ideas in a variety of contexts. Using prompt engineering techniques, SMEs can integrate AI into their innovation processes, test hypothetical scenarios and enrich their brainstorming sessions. With simulated role-playing, automatically generated product ideas and impact assessments, AI becomes a true strategic partner to help companies push back the boundaries of innovation.

CHAPTER 8

PERFORMING MACHINE LEARNING WITH CHATGPT USING PROMPTS ONLY

Chapter objective: This chapter explains how to use ChatGPT to carry out a complete machine learning project, from analysing data to making predictions, using only prompts. You won't need to write a single line of code; it's all done through simple interactions with ChatGPT. We will cover three practical examples based on available datasets: regression, classification, and clustering. By the end of this chapter, you'll be able to do machine learning and use models to make live predictions.

8.1 Introduction to Machine Learning with ChatGPT

Machine learning is a branch of artificial intelligence that enables computers to learn from data and make decisions or predictions without being explicitly programmed for each task. This capability is particularly useful for solving complex problems such as predicting sales, segmenting customers or identifying patterns of behaviour in large datasets.

DIFFERENCES BETWEEN MACHINE LEARNING AND TRADITIONAL MATHEMATICS

• Nature of the data: Machine learning works well with complex, unstructured data (such as images or text), whereas traditional mathematics focuses mainly on structured data.
• Data-driven resolution: In machine learning, the model

"learns' from the data and adjusts its parameters to minimise the errors. In traditional mathematics, resolution is determined by fixed formulae.
• Probability vs. determinism: Machine learning predictions are often probabilistic (e.g. "there is a 90% chance that this customer will buy this product"), whereas traditional mathematics aims for deterministic results.

Machine learning is based on algorithms that can analyse patterns hidden in the data and adapt to make more accurate predictions as they are exposed to new data.

8.2 The stages of a Machine Learning project with ChatGPT

Here are the main steps to successfully complete a machine learning project with ChatGPT :

1. Data preparation: Understanding the structure of the data, analysing distributions and identifying important variables.
2. Choice of algorithm: Test several algorithms (regression, classification, clustering) to choose the one offering the best performance.
3. Performance evaluation: Use metrics such as precision, recall and F1 score to assess model quality.
4. Live predictions: Use the selected model to make predictions based on new data vectors.

8.3 Practical Example 1: Monthly Sales Prediction (Regression)

BACKGROUND

We want to predict the monthly sales of a product as a function of advertising expenditure and the price of the product. The aim is to identify how variations in these two variables affect sales and to find a model capable of predicting future sales.

Data file : Download the monthly sales dataset

STEP 1: ANALYSE THE DATA

Prompt :

```
ChatGPT, here's a file of monthly sales data which includes the columns
"Month", "Advertising_Spend", "Product_Price", and "Sales". Can you
analyse this data and give me an overview of the descriptive statistics?
```

Expected answer :

- ChatGPT provides a summary of the descriptive statistics, showing the means, standard deviations, minima and maxima for each variable.
- It could also visualise the relationship between advertising expenditure and sales to show the impact of each variable.

STEP 2: FINDING THE BEST REGRESSION MODEL

Prompt :

Test several regression models (linear regression, ridge regression, lasso regression) and tell me which one performs best using the coefficient of determination (R^2) and the mean square error (MSE).

Expected answer :

• ChatGPT tests each model, gives the R^2 and MSE scores for each model, and recommends the model with the best performance.

STEP 3 : USE THE MODEL FOR MAKE PREDICTIONS

Prompt :

```
Use the selected linear regression model to predict monthly sales if
advertising expenditure is €2,500 and the product price is €22. What would
be the predicted sales?
```

Expected answer :

• ChatGPT uses the model to predict sales and returns a figure, for example: Predicted sales would be 780 units.

8.4 Practical example 2: Customer segmentation (Classification)

BACKGROUND

We want to segment customers into several groups ('low income', 'middle income', 'high income') based on their age, annual income and spending score. The aim is to understand customer behaviour and optimise marketing campaigns.

Data file: Download the customer segmentation dataset

STEP 1: ANALYSE THE DATA

Prompt :

```
ChatGPT, here's a customer segmentation data file which includes the
columns "Age", "Annual_Income", "Spending_Score", and "Segment". Can you
analyse this data and give me an overview of the distributions for each
variable?
```

Expected answer :

• ChatGPT provides an overview of the distribution of ages, incomes and spending scores. It also identifies the distribution of customers in each segment.

STEP 2 : CHOOSE THE BEST ALGORITHM CLASSIFICATION ALGORITHM

Prompt :

```
Test several classification models (K-Nearest Neighbors, Decision Tree, SVM)
and tell me which one performs best using accuracy and F1 score. Which one
should we use for customer segmentation?
```

Expected response:

• ChatGPT evaluates each model, returns accuracy and F1 scores, and recommends the model that best segments customers.

STEP 3 : USE THE MODEL FOR MAKE PREDICTIONS

Prompt :

```
Use the selected model to predict the customer segment for a customer with
an age of 34, an annual income of €70,000 and an expenditure score of 65.
```

Expected response:

• ChatGPT uses the model to predict the segment, for example: The customer belongs to the "Average income" segment.

8.5 Practical example 3: Identifying behavioural segments (clustering)

BACKGROUND

We want to identify groups of customers with similar buying behaviours. We're going to use clustering to group customers by age, annual income and spending score to better understand their habits.

Data file: Download the clustering dataset

STEP 1: ANALYSE THE DATA

Prompt :

```
ChatGPT, here's a shopping behaviour data file which includes the columns
"Age", "Annual_Income", and "Spending_Score". Can you give me an analysis of
the distribution of these variables?
```

Expected response:

• ChatGPT provides an overview of the distribution of variables and identifies possible patterns of behaviour.

STEP 2: IDENTIFY BEHAVIOURAL SEGMENTS

Prompt :

```
Use clustering algorithms (K-Means, DBSCAN) to identify segments of
behaviour. Tell me how many clusters are identified and describe each
segment.
```

Expected answer :

- ChatGPT performs the clustering, identifies the optimal number of clusters and provides a description of each segment.

STEP 3 : USE THE SEGMENTS FORBETTER UNDERSTAND CUSTOMERS

Prompt :

```
Which segment does a 45-year-old customer with an annual income of €90,000
and an expenditure score of 75 belong to?
```

Expected answer :

- ChatGPT uses the clustering model to assign the customer to a segment, for example: The customer belongs to the "High Income Buyers" segment.

Conclusion: Using ChatGPT for Machine Learning Projects without Writing Code

ChatGPT is a powerful tool for carrying out machine learning projects using only prompts. You can analyse data, test several models, identify the best algorithm and make predictions without any programming knowledge. Thanks to the datasets provided, you can put these concepts into practice and discover how to use AI to improve your decision-making and strategic processes.Download the datasets and experiment with the prompts provided to create your own machine learning project interacting directly with ChatGPT.

CHAPTER 9

AUTOMATING PREDICTIONS AND REPETITIVE TASKS WITH CHATGPT

Chapter objective: This chapter explores how ChatGPT can be used to automate predictions based on machine learning models and perform repetitive tasks within SMEs. We will show how AI can be integrated into business workflows to generate daily predictions, automate decision making and create automatic reports. Through case studies, you will see how to set up automatic processes using only ChatGPT interactions, without writing any code.

9.1 Automation with ChatGPT: Advantages and Opportunities

Automating repetitive tasks and predictions is a major opportunity for SMEs. It reduces the workload of employees, improves the accuracy of operations and frees up time for higher value-added activities. ChatGPT, combined with machine learning models, can automate processes such as creating reports, generating forecasts and even making decisions.

Benefits of automation with ChatGPT :

1. Time savings: repetitive tasks such as creating reports or analysing trends can be automated, reducing the time spent on these activities.
2. Increased accuracy: Machine learning models offer accurate predictions and data-driven analysis.
3. Error reduction: Automated processes minimise human error.
4. Speed of reaction: Automation enables decisions to be taken more quickly in response to events or changes in the market.

9.2 Automating Sales Predictions : A Case Study

BACKGROUND

We trained a regression model to predict monthly sales based on advertising spend and product price. The model can now be integrated into an automated workflow to make predictions each month and send automatic reports by email.

STEP 1: PREPARING TO AUTOMATE PREDICTIONS

Prompt :

```
ChatGPT, I'd like to automate monthly sales predictions using ad spend and
product pricing data. Can you set up a workflow that takes in new data each
month, makes the predictions, and sends an automatic report to my email?
```

Expected answer :

• ChatGPT shows you how to set up an automation workflow. This could include using a cloud storage service to load the new monthly data, ChatGPT to make the predictions and an automated email service (such as Zapier or a Python script using smtplib) to send the report.

STEP 2: SIMULATE THE AUTOMATION FLOW

Prompt :

```
Let's assume that the new data for this month are: Advertising
expenditure = €3,000, Product price = €22. Use the regression
model to predict monthly sales and generate a summary report.
```

Expected answer :

• ChatGPT uses the new data, applies the regression model and generates a report showing the predicted amount of sales, the variations compared with the previous month, and a recommendation (for example, to increase or reduce advertising expenditure).

STEP 3: AUTOMATE THE SENDING OF REPORTS

Prompt :

```
Based on the monthly predictions, generate a report and send it automatically
to the email address marketing@example.com each month. Can you guide me
through this automation?
```

Expected answer :

• ChatGPT offers a step-by-step guide to integrating this flow with an email service such as Gmail or an RPA (Robotic Process Automation) tool.

9.3 Automated Prediction of Customer Behaviour CONTEXT

Using classification or clustering models, it is possible to identify customer segments that are most likely to make a purchase, leave the service, or respond positively to a marketing campaign. Once the model has been trained, automation can be used to predict these behaviours on a weekly or monthly basis and generate automatic recommendations.

STEP 1: CONFIGURING BEHAVIOURAL ANALYSIS

Prompt :

```
ChatGPT, I'd like to set up an automatic analysis of customer behaviour to
identify high-potential segments. Can you guide me through setting up a
weekly analysis that predicts which customer segments to target?
```

Expected answer :

- ChatGPT offers a workflow that uses the clustering model to analyse the behaviour of each segment on a weekly basis and generate priority segment reports.

STEP 2: SIMULATING BEHAVIOUR PREDICTIONS

Prompt :

```
For this week, here is the customer data: Age = 34, Annual income = €75,000,
Spend score = 70. Use the clustering model to identify this customer's
segment and recommend a marketing action.
```

Expected answer :

- ChatGPT identifies the customer segment (e.g. Regular Buyers) and proposes an action (e.g. Send a special offer to increase the average basket).

9.4 Automated creation of weekly reports

BACKGROUND

In many companies, weekly reports (on sales, team performance or customer behaviour) are generated manually. ChatGPT can automate this task, bring together the data from different sources, generate graphs and tables, and automatically send reports to stakeholders.

STEP 1: CONFIGURING A REPORT TEMPLATE

Prompt :

```
ChatGPT, I'd like to automate the creation of weekly sales performance
reports. Can you set up a report template that includes sales, weekly
variations and an analysis of performance by product?
```

Expected answer :

• ChatGPT provides a report template with the following sections:

o Summary of weekly sales.

o Analysis of the best-performing products.

o Recommendations for the following week.

STEP 2: GENERATE A REPORT AUTOMATICALLY

Prompt :

```
Using this week's data (Sales = €7,000, Product A = €2,000, Product B =
€1,500, etc.), generate an automatic report with performance graphs and
recommendations for the following week.
```

Expected answer :

• ChatGPT generates a comprehensive report incorporating graphs, trends and performance-based recommendations.

STEP 3: AUTOMATE THE SENDING OF REPORTS

Prompt :

```
Configure this weekly report to be sent automatically to the sales team email
address (sales_team@example.com) every Monday morning.
```

Expected answer :

• ChatGPT offers a guide to integrating this process with an automated emailing service (for example, using Zapier to trigger sending every Monday morning).

9.5 Using ChatGPT for Automated Decision Making

ChatGPT can also be used to automate data-driven decision-making. For example, a machine learning model can predict which stocks to replenish, which customers to contact or which campaigns to launch based on the results obtained.

Prompt :

```
ChatGPT, I want to set up an automated decision-making workflow. Based on
sales predictions, automatically decide whether we need to increase or
reduce stock for each product. Can you give me a plan for this automation?
```

Expected answer :

- ChatGPT offers a workflow with the following steps:

1. Collect sales forecasts.
2. Compare with current stocks.
3. Make a decision (increase, reduce or maintain stock).
4. Generate automatic recommendations.

9.6 Conclusion: Automating Repetitive Tasks with ChatGPT to Increase Efficiency

This chapter has shown how ChatGPT can be used to automate repetitive tasks such as monthly predictions, customer behaviour analysis and reporting. By integrating ChatGPT into automated workflows, SMEs can increase efficiency, reduce errors, and improve decision-making. Use the prompts provided to create your own workflows and unlock the potential of AI in your business.

CHAPTER 10

PLANNING AND IMPLEMENTING AN AI INTEGRATION STRATEGY IN SMES

Chapter objective: This chapter provides a practical and structured guide for SMEs wishing to integrate artificial intelligence (AI) into their business. We will cover the essential steps for planning, preparing and implementing an AI integration strategy tailored to the size, needs and resources available within SMEs. Concrete examples will illustrate each step, from defining objectives to assessing impact.

10.1 Why integrate AI into an SME?

The integration of AI is no longer the preserve of large companies. More and more SMEs are adopting artificial intelligence technologies to optimise their processes, improve customer satisfaction and stand out from the competition. However, the adoption of AI needs to be carefully considered and structured in order to maximise the benefits while minimising the risks.

Benefits of integrating AI in an SME :

1. Automate repetitive tasks: Reduce the time spent on manual tasks such as email management, order processing or data entry.
2. Improved decision-making: using predictive analysis to anticipate market trends, customer demand and financial flows.
3. Resource optimisation: more efficient allocation of human and financial resources thanks to recommendations based on machine learning models.
4. Personalised customer experience: using AI to analyse customer behaviour and propose personalised offers.

Example: An SME in the retail sector uses AI to predict demand for its products, thereby reducing storage costs and increasing the availability of the most popular items.

10.2 Assessing the Needs and Defining the Objectives of AI Integration

Before integrating AI, it is crucial to identify the company's specific needs and define clear, measurable objectives. This will enable the right technologies to be selected and an implementation roadmap to be drawn up that is tailored to the company's capabilities.

STEP 1: IDENTIFY OPPORTUNITIES FOR INTEGRATING IA

Start by assessing current processes and identifying those that could benefit from AI. Typical areas where AI can be integrated include:

- Customer Relationship Management (CRM): Automation of customer responses, customer segmentation for targeted marketing campaigns.
- Logistics and supply chain: Demand forecasting, stock optimisation.
- Finance: analysis of cash flows, prediction of financial trends.
- Human resources: Analysis of job applications, employee satisfaction management.

Prompt Suggestion for ChatGPT :

```
ChatGPT, help me identify the processes within my SME that could benefit
from AI integration. I'd like to know which areas have the most potential
for automation or advanced analytics.
```

Expected answer :

- ChatGPT offers a list of the most relevant processes for integrating AI, depending on the nature of the business (for example, automated email processing for customer service, analysis of sales data to optimise stocks, etc.).

STEP 2: DEFINE CLEAR, MEASURABLE OBJECTIVES

Objectives should be aligned with the company's strategic priorities and include key performance indicators (KPIs). Examples of objectives:

- Reduce labour costs by 20% by automating administrative tasks.
- Increase sales by 15% using predictive models for marketing targeting.
- Reduce the churn rate (customer attrition) by 10% by personalising the customer experience.

Prompt Suggestion for ChatGPT :

```
Can you help me define clear and measurable objectives for integrating AI
into my SME? I want to prioritise the automation of administrative tasks and
improve customer satisfaction.
```

Expected answer :

- ChatGPT proposes specific objectives, such as Automate 50% of data entry tasks within 6 months or Increase customer satisfaction score by 10 points in one year.

10.3 Choosing the right AI Technologies and Models

The choice of AI technologies and models to be used depends on the objectives defined. It is important to select solutions that can be easily integrated into existing systems and that are scalable.

CHOOSING BETWEEN OFF-THE-SHELF TECHNOLOGIES AND CUSTOM DEVELOPMENT

1. Ready-to-use solutions (SaaS): Use existing AI platforms such as intelligent CRM, chatbots or predictive analysis tools. These solutions are easy to integrate and do not require advanced technical skills.
   - Examples: Zendesk for automated customer support, HubSpot for marketing automation.
2. Tailor-made development: create customised models based on the company's specific needs (e.g. neural networks for demand prediction, clustering models for customer segmentation).
   - Examples: Machine learning models with Scikit-Learn, TensorFlow or PyTorch.

Prompt Suggestion for ChatGPT :

```
ChatGPT, should I use an out-of-the-box AI solution for my customer service
or develop a custom model? Here are the specifics of my business...
```

Expected answer :

- ChatGPT analyses requirements and recommends the best solution based on the complexity of the tasks and the available budget.

10.4 Drawing up an AI Implementation Roadmap

A clear roadmap helps to structure the project and define the key stages in integrating AI into the company. This roadmap should include:

1. Current state analysis: Mapping of existing processes.
2. Definition of priorities: Identification of the processes to be automated first.
3. Technology selection: Choice of AI tools and platforms.
4. Phased deployment: Gradual implementation with pilots on isolated processes.
5. Evaluation and adjustment: Ongoing evaluation of performance and adjustment of strategy

based on results.

Example of a Roadmap :

Step	Activity	Duration	Manager
1. Analysis of current situation	Map processes and identify opportunities	2 weeks	Project manager
2. Setting priorities	Prioritise the processes to be automated	1 week	Team
3.Select of technologies	Evaluate the tools available and choose the solutions	3 weeks	IT Team
4. Pilot deployment	Implement a pilot project on a key process	4 weeks	Technical team
5. Evaluation	Measuring performance and adjusting strategy	Continuous	Team

10.5 Overcoming the Challenges of AI Integration (Continued)

For AI integration to be successful, it is crucial to consider the potential challenges that SMEs could face. Here's how to overcome the main obstacles:

RESISTANCE TO ORGANISATIONAL CHANGE

Employees may feel threatened by the introduction of AI, fearing excessive automation or job loss. To overcome this resistance, it is important to :

- Clearly communicate the objectives: Explain how AI can help them in their work and not replace them.
- Involve teams from the outset: Employees need to be involved in discussions and understand the benefits for themselves and the company.
- Train staff: Organise training sessions to improve their understanding of AI and develop their skills in digital technologies.

Prompt Suggestion for ChatGPT :

```
ChatGPT, what strategies should I use to overcome employee resistance to the
integration of AI into my business? How can I reassure them about their
future role?
```

Expected answer :

- ChatGPT offers communication and training strategies, as well as concrete actions to involve employees, such as setting up collaborative workshops and feedback sessions.

LACK OF DATA

AI is only as good as the data it is trained on. Insufficient or poor quality data can adversely affect model performance.

Solutions:

1. Collect more data: Use forms, surveys or IoT devices to enrich internal data.
2. Increase data quality: Clean data to eliminate outliers, duplicates and errors.
3. Use external data: Integrate third-party APIs to access market or demographic data.

Prompt Suggestion for ChatGPT :

```
ChatGPT, how can I collect more relevant data to train my machine learning
models? What types of data should I prioritise?
```

Expected response:

• ChatGPT identifies potential data sources (e.g. customer data, market trends) and suggests suitable collection methods, such as integrating external APIs or working with partners.

TECHNICAL COMPLEXITY AND LACK OF SKILLS

SMEs may encounter technical difficulties due to the complexity of AI models and the lack of qualified personnel.

Solutions:

1. Train in-house staff: Organise training in machine learning and AI development.
2. Collaborate with external partners: work with AI consultants or technology start-ups.
3. Use simplified AI platforms: Choose platforms with user-friendly interfaces (e.g. AutoML) that require few coding skills.

Prompt Suggestion for ChatGPT :

```
ChatGPT, my team doesn't have advanced AI skills. What tools or platforms
should we use to facilitate the integration of AI without technical
expertise?
```

Expected response:

• ChatGPT recommends tools such as Google AutoML, DataRobot and H2O.ai, which simplify the development and integration of machine learning models.

10.6 Evaluating and adjusting the AI Integration Strategy

Once AI has been implemented, it is essential to monitor its impact on business performance and make adjustments based on the results obtained.

MEASURING THE IMPACT OF IA

To assess the effectiveness of the AI integration strategy, it is advisable to monitor several key performance indicators (KPIs):

1. Operational efficiency :
   - o Reduced processing times.
   - o Lower production costs.
   - o Number of automated tasks.
2. Customer and employee satisfaction:
   - o Improved customer satisfaction scores (NPS, retention rate).
   - o Positive feedback on AI from employees.
3. Return on investment (ROI) :
   - o Measure the savings achieved (e.g. reduction in costs linked to errors or delays).
   - o Gains achieved through increased sales or optimisation of resources.

ADJUST THE STRATEGY IN LINE WITH RESULTS

Once the results have been collected and analysed, it is important to adjust the strategy in line with performance:

- If the results are positive: Extend the use of AI to other business processes.
- If results are mixed: Identify the sources of poor performance (e.g. lack of data, poorly adapted model) and adjust the project.
- If the results are negative: Review the initial objectives and reassess the suitability of AI for the process in question.

Prompt Suggestion for ChatGPT :

```
ChatGPT, how should I evaluate the performance of the AI implemented in my
company? What are the most relevant indicators to monitor?
```

Expected answer :

• ChatGPT recommends monitoring KPIs specific to the AI objective (e.g. effectiveness, cost, satisfaction) and suggests methods for adjusting the strategy in the event of unexpected results.

10.7 Extending the Use of AI in Other Business Processes

Once AI is well established in the company's key processes, its use can be extended to other departments:

1. Marketing: Using AI to analyse customer behaviour, automate advertising campaigns and personalise offers.
2. Sales: Integrate AI-based recommendation tools to offer complementary products.
3. Human resources: Automate the sorting of applications, assess employee sentiment and forecast training needs.

Example: An SME that has automated its customer service with an AI-based chatbot decides to extend this technology to the analysis of customer feedback to identify areas for product improvement.

Prompt Suggestion for ChatGPT :

ChatGPT, now that AI is well integrated into our stock management, what other departments could benefit from this technology? Can you give me some examples?

Expected answer :

• ChatGPT identifies other application areas for AI, such as accounting (cash flow prediction), marketing (advanced customer segmentation) and sales (product recommendations based on purchase data).

Case study: Developing a comprehensive AI integration strategy

BACKGROUND

An SME in the distribution sector wants to use AI to optimise its operations, improve the customer experience and predict sales trends. Here are the key steps for implementing a comprehensive AI integration strategy.

STEP 1: MAP PROCESSES AND IDENTIFY OPPORTUNITIES

Define key processes, identify inefficiencies and establish priorities.

Prompt Suggestion:

```
ChatGPT, can you help me map my SME's key processes and identify those
that are priorities for AI? I want to target the processes that consume
the most resources.
```

STEP 2: DEFINING OBJECTIVES AND SELECTING TECHNOLOGIES

Choose the AI integration objectives (e.g. reduce the cost of stock management by 15%) and select the appropriate tools (e.g. predictive models for stocks).

Prompt Suggestion:

```
What objectives should I set to optimise my stock management with AI? Can
you also recommend suitable technologies?
```

STAGE 3: ROLL OUT THE IA GRADUALLY

Start with pilot projects on isolated processes, evaluate performance and adjust before rolling out on a large scale.

Prompt Suggestion:

```
What plan should I follow to deploy AI gradually? What success criteria
should I follow at each stage?
```

STAGE 4: MEASURING IMPACT AND EVALUATING RESULTS

Monitor the defined KPIs and adjust the strategy according to the results obtained.

Prompt Suggestion:

```
How should I assess the impact of AI on my company's performance?
? What KPIs should I be keeping a close eye on?
```

Conclusion: Developing a Successful AI Integration Strategy

Integrating AI into an SME requires careful planning, selection of the right technologies and gradual implementation. By following the steps outlined in this chapter, you will be able to create an AI strategy aligned with your business objectives, ensure successful adoption, and measure its impact to adjust your approach.

REFERENCES

4. Ng, A. (2021). The AI Transformation Playbook: How AI Changes the Business Landscape. McKinsey & Company.

5. Russell, S., & Norvig, P. (2020). Artificial Intelligence: A Modern Approach. Prentice Hall.

6. Goodfellow, I., Bengio, Y., & Courville, A. (2016). Deep Learning. MIT Press.

7. Bughin, J., Hazan, E., & Ramaswamy, S. (2017). "Artificial Intelligence: The Next Digital Frontier?" McKinsey Global Institute.

8. Kumar, A., & Mehta, S. (2019). AI in Customer Service: Chatbots and Beyond. Springer.

9. Davenport, T. H., & Ronanki, R. (2018). "Artificial Intelligence for the Real World". Harvard Business Review, 96(1).

10. Kim, J., & Hwang, C. (2020). AI-Powered E-commerce: How AI Transforms the Digital Shopping Experience. Wiley.

11. Brown, T. B., et al. (2020). "Language Models are Few-Shot Learners". Advances in Neural Information Processing Systems.

12. Vaswani, A., et al. (2017). "Attention Is All You Need". Advances in Neural Information Processing Systems.

13. OpenAI (2020). GPT-3 Technical Paper. OpenAI.

14. McCarthy, J., et al. (2018). The AI Design Handbook. O'Reilly Media.

15. Dean, J. (2019). "Building and Scaling AI for the Enterprise". Google Cloud Blog.

16. Scikit-Learn Documentation - Linear Regression. Available at: https://scikit-learn.org/stable/modules/generated/sklearn.linear_model.LinearRegression.html.

17. Scikit-Learn Documentation - K-Nearest Neighbors. Available at: https://scikit-learn.org/stable/modules/neighbors.html.

18. Scikit-Learn Documentation - Vector Machine Support. Available at: https://scikit-learn.org/stable/modules/svm.html.

19. Scikit-Learn Documentation - Decision Trees. Available at: https://scikit-learn.org/stable/modules/tree.html.

20. Scikit-Learn Documentation - Random Forest. Available at: https://scikit-learn.org/stable/modules/ensemble.html.

21. Scikit-Learn Documentation - Logistic Regression. Available at: https://scikit-learn.org/stable/modules/generated/sklearn.linear_model.LogisticRegression.html.

22. TensorFlow Documentation - Introduction to Machine Learning with TensorFlow. Available

at: https://www.tensorflow.org/tutorials.
23. "An Introduction to Clustering with K-Means" by A. Ng, Coursera. Available at: https://www.coursera.org/learn/machine-learning.
24. "Machine Learning Yearning" by Andrew Ng. Available at: https://www.deeplearning.ai/machine-learning-yearning/.
25. "Python Data Science Handbook" by Jake VanderPlas. Available at: https://jakevdp.github.io/PythonDataScienceHandbook/.
26. Google AI Blog - "Understanding Machine Learning". Available at: https://ai.googleblog.com/.
27. "Hands-On Machine Learning with Scikit-Learn, Keras, and TensorFlow" by Aurélien Géron. O'Reilly Media, 2019.
28. "Pattern Recognition and Machine Learning" by Christopher Bishop. Springer, 2006.

TABLE OF CONTENTS

MIX
Papier aus verantwortungsvollen Quellen
Paper from responsible sources
FSC® C105338

Printed by Books on Demand GmbH, Norderstedt / Germany